Look, My Little Counting Book

Tickle My Tummy, Look and Learn Series

Book Three

Written and Illustrated by

Ali C. Johnson

WestBow Press books may be ordered through booksellers or by contacting:

WestBow Press
A Division of Thomas Nelson & Zondervan
1663 Liberty Drive
Bloomington, IN 47403
www.westbowpress.com
1 (866) 928-1240

ISBN: 978-1-4908-8265-9 (sc)
ISBN: 978-1-4908-8266-6 (e)

Library of Congress Control Number: 2015908630

Print information available on the last page.

WestBow Press rev. date: 07/16/2015

WESTBOW PRESS®
A DIVISION OF THOMAS NELSON & ZONDERVAN

This little book belongs to:

Look,
one, two, three, four,
all the monkeys on the
grassy floor!

Five, six, seven, eight, all the monkeys out the gate.

Oh me, oh my, nine and ten;
won't you count them
all again?

Oh, no! Where did they go?
The two littlest monkeys,
Don't you know?

Look,
past the traffic lights,
one, two, three.

Run, run, down the street.
Wee! Wee! Wee!

Look,
what a fuss, all the monkeys
on the bus!

Help! Help! Call 911!
Bring a banana for everyone.

Look,
How many bananas might there be?
Count every one that you can see.

Look,
the zookeeper shouted as he
jumped up and down,
you precious little monkeys,
gather all around.

All along the street, a
trail is left behind, just for the
monkeys to happily find.

One, two, three, four, five, six,
seven, eight,
as they follow the zookeeper
through the gate.

Look!
The smallest little monkeys
nine and ten;

Now safe and sound in the zoo again!

The End

A message to you from a grandmother's heart; God has put the desire for greatness in each of our hearts. Think big, and let your imagination soar! Your potential has no limits. Go for it!

Ali C. Johnson resides in northern Minnesota, with her husband, children and grandchildren. She loves every moment shared with her growing family. Time spent telling stories and writing poems for her little ones has been the inspiration to share them with other children to enjoy.

www.ingramcontent.com/pod-product-compliance
Ingram Content Group UK Ltd.
Pitfield, Milton Keynes, MK11 3LW, UK
UKHW061950290726
14090UKWH00021B/1158

9 781490 882659